HOW CAN I
SERVE GOD AT WORK?

✗ Cultivating Biblical Godliness

Series Editors

Joel R. Beeke and Ryan M. McGraw

Dr. D. Martyn Lloyd-Jones once said that what the church needs to do most of all is "to begin herself to live the Christian life. If she did that, men and women would be crowding into our buildings. They would say, 'What is the secret of this?'" As Christians, one of our greatest needs is for the Spirit of God to cultivate biblical godliness in us in order to put the beauty of Christ on display through us, all to the glory of the triune God. With this goal in mind, this series of booklets treats matters vital to Christian experience at a basic level. Each booklet addresses a specific question in order to inform the mind, warm the affections, and transform the whole person by the Spirit's grace, so that the church may adorn the doctrine of God our Savior in all things.

HOW CAN I
SERVE GOD AT WORK?

RAY PENNINGS

REFORMATION HERITAGE BOOKS
GRAND RAPIDS, MICHIGAN

Reformation Heritage Books
2965 Leonard St. NE
Grand Rapids, MI 49525
616-977-0889 / Fax 616-285-3246
orders@heritagebooks.org
www.heritagebooks.org

Printed in the United States of America
17 18 19 20 21 22/10 9 8 7 6 5 4 3 2 1

ISBN 978-1-60178-549-7

*For additional Reformed literature, request a free book list from
Reformation Heritage Books at the above regular or e-mail address.*

HOW CAN I
SERVE GOD AT WORK?

————————✕————————

In his famous *Treatise of the Vocations*, the Puritan William Perkins defined vocation as "a certain kind of life, ordained or imposed on man by God, for the common good."[1] Perkins described this idea as countercultural in his sixteenth-century context, when a "common saying [was] *Every man for himself and God for us all*." This thinking, Perkins said, was "wicked" and "directly against the end of every calling or honest kind of life."[2] Now, four and a half centuries later, his words are as relevant as they were then.

We naturally think that our work is about us. To use our individual gifts, we need to take inventory of them. Few of us manage to do so without succumbing either to pride or to covetousness and, in many

---

1. Portions of this booklet are adapted from Ray Pennings, "Working for God's Glory," in Joel R. Beeke, *Living for God's Glory: An Introduction to Calvinism* (Lake Mary, Fla.: Reformation Trust, 2008).

2. William Perkins, *A Treatise of the Vocations or Callings of men, with sorts and kinds of them, and the right use thereof* (London: John Legatt, 1626), http://bit.ly/2vN19A3.

cases, both. We celebrate what we are able to do well, and from our earliest age we compare ourselves to those around us. Already on the playground, someone is smarter, faster, or quicker. Others are less so. When we enter the workforce, we attach dollars and authority to these gifts. Each society, and indeed each workplace, develops a value system, and, depending on how we fit in, we prosper or not, as the case may be. Whether it is in the assessment of our own gifts or of those of our coworkers, tension and difference of opinion is common. If loving God above all and our neighbor as ourselves is the summary of the law (Matt. 22:37–40), most of us will readily admit that the workplace is an especially difficult place to obey it.

But the road to a biblical perspective on work has two ditches. Misevaluating or misdirecting the good gifts that God has provided is one. But there is also the uncomfortable reality that in the workplace, the curse on sin comes to particular expression. "In the sweat of thy face shalt thou eat bread, till thou return unto the ground," God told Adam after the fall (Gen. 3:19). All Adam's offspring know something of labor's toil. Literal and figurative thorns and thistles prick us daily. The weeds of workplace stuff easily crowd out the good plants that we are trying to cultivate in our vocational endeavors. Tedium, stress, and fatigue are part of our work experience.

Depending on how you do the math (and the extent to which we succumb to either the sin of sloth or workaholism), most of us spend between one-third and one-half of our waking lives working. The Reformation recovered the biblical truth that regardless of our vocation, the gospel impacts our work. Whereas the Roman Catholic Church made a stark distinction between sacred and secular professions, with the common folk having a clear perception that God received greater glory from the work of a priest or monk than from a farmer or carpenter, the Reformation resisted that distortion. "The action of a shepherd in keeping sheep, performed as I have said, in his kind, is as good a work before God as the action of a judge in giving sentence; or a Magistrate in ruling, or a Minister in preaching," wrote Perkins.[3] Os Guinness summarizes this well:

> For Martin Luther and subsequent reformers, the recovery of the holistic understanding of calling was dramatic. Writing about the "Estate of Marriage" in 1522, Luther declared that God and the angels smile when a man changes a diaper. William Tyndale wrote that, if our desire is to please God, pouring water, washing dishes, cobbling shoes, and preaching the Word "is all one." William Perkins claimed polishing shoes was a sanctified and holy act. John Milton wrote in *Paradise Lost*:
>
>> To know
>> That which before us lies in daily life
>> Is the Prime Wisdom.

---

3. Perkins, *Treatise of Vocations*, 18.

Bishop Thomas Becon wrote, "Our Saviour Christ was a carpenter. His apostles were fishermen. St. Paul was a tent-maker."[4]

Experiencing communion with God in the course of everyday duty may seem unreasonably idealistic. Yet, as the apostle Paul reminds the Galatians, the life of faith is experienced *in the flesh*: "I am crucified with Christ: nevertheless I live; yet not I, but Christ liveth in me: and the life which I now live in the flesh I live by the faith of the Son of God, who loved me, and gave himself for me" (2:20). Knowing that her beloved Bridegroom purchased the world in which she does her daily work, the bride delights as she finds new reasons every day to delight in and praise her Groom. The Groom also delights in the worship of the bride, not just in anticipation of the future they will have together, but already now, in real time. Yes, the bride lives a real, earthly life, doing physical and mental things in real time, but with Christ living in her, she experiences spiritual satisfaction and communion with her Beloved, rejoicing with Him regarding things that she knows He delights in. We can be sure that whatever part of God's creation our occupation gives us to engage, the God who "delights" in a working scale (Prov.

---

4. Os Guinness, *The Call: Finding and Fulfilling the Central Purpose of Your Life* (New York: W Publishing Group, 1998), 16–17.

11:1) is more knowledgeable about and interested in it than we are.

This booklet seeks to unpack what this might mean for believers seeking to cultivate everyday godliness in a twenty-first-century North American context. It is organized around ten principles summarizing biblical teaching that, taken in combination, might be thought of as "Theology of Work 101." Inundated as we are with secular distortions regarding how to think about our work lives, it is necessary to remind ourselves of basic scriptural truths in order that we think clearly about the subject. Then, I will briefly touch on how a biblical view of vocation contrasts with a secular one and how this might make a difference as we head to work in the morning. I pray that readers will find helpful encouragement and instruction and that God's people might be better equipped to serve and glorify Him in how they deal with what are sometimes considered less spiritual matters.

WHAT IS WORK?

What exactly do I mean by *work*? The term is broader than the terms *job* or *labor*. Those terms refer to our livelihood, those tasks that we do from which we derive our income. The term *work* refers to something broader—to "all that we are obliged to do to meet our physical and social needs,"[5] as one author puts it. *Webster's Dictionary* similarly struggles to define the word precisely, highlighting how many different ways the word is used but offering the most precision when it says that work is "effort directed toward some purpose or end." The dimensions of work are many. Each of us could provide different descriptions of our work that might focus on the physical, mental, emotional, social, economic, psychological, ethical, or legal aspect of it—and that list is hardly complete. I could further complicate matters by considering the place in which work occurs, recognizing that the context for work is very different in contemporary North America than it would be in Africa or South America. I also recognize that we cannot separate our experience and understanding of work from the economic and political structures within which work takes place—how we are treated in the workplace and the manner in which such lofty concepts including justice, power, and authority are exercised. As real as all of these are, they go beyond my scope here, even as I acknowledge that what is covered in this booklet can't really be applied without regard to the setting in which our work takes place.

Rather, I will focus on the narrow concept of work itself, recognizing that while we think of these things with reference to a formal workplace, the

---

5. Leland Ryken, *Redeeming the Time: A Christian Approach to Work and Leisure* (Grand Rapids: Baker, 1995), 16.

principles are equally applicable to whatever occupies our time in our present stage of life. You might be a student whose present work is completing a formal program of study at an educational institution, a homemaker caring for children, a volunteer or a retiree—your present work is fulfilling the set of tasks that is expected of you each day.

I will briefly discuss the biblical concept of vocation (you may recognize the Latin root *vocare*, meaning "to call") toward the end of this booklet, but it is helpful to remind ourselves of the comfort that the doctrine of God's sovereignty and providence provides. Whatever stage of life in which you find yourself, there is work for you to do each day that has meaning before God. While many of our tasks have utilitarian consequences of which we are appropriately conscious, there is meaning in what you do apart from the consequences. Being a diligent student may get you good grades and the diploma that qualifies you for a desired career, but being a diligent student matters today, regardless of what grade or diploma you earn, because God receives more glory by you being a diligent student than a slothful one. Providing excellent goods or services to your customers may advance your career, but even more importantly, it glorifies God: "And whatsoever ye do, do it heartily, as to the Lord, and not unto men" (Col. 3:23).

There is little doubt that our views on work are affected by the culture in which we live. Christian sociologist James Davison Hunter notes, based on a survey of students enrolled at Christian colleges and seminaries, that in the evangelical world, "work has lost any spiritual and eternal significance and that it is important only insofar as it fosters certain qualities of the personality."[6] Insofar as Christians have a distinct view of work, that view is usually driven by ethical considerations. "Be honest; don't steal from your employer; don't participate in the temptations of the workplace," is advice that is often given. It is valid advice. Christians are to demonstrate the fruits of the Spirit in workplace relationships.

But I want to get beyond that in this booklet. Being ethical in our work deserves attention, but for our purposes here, I am taking for granted that we agree that we are called to be honest, loving, and exemplary in every aspect of our lives—at home, in church, with our friends and neighbors, and at work. My focus is not as much on Christians in the workplace as it is on a Christian perspective of work. The distinction is an important one. Perkins summarized this well: "Adam in his innocence had all things at his will, yet then God employed him in a calling; therefore none must be exempted, but every man both high and low must walk in his proper calling."[7]

God is more glorified by a job well done than by one poorly done. A well-chaired meeting is

<hr />

6. James Davison Hunter, *Evangelicalism: The Coming Generation* (Chicago: University of Chicago Press, 1987), 56.

7. As quoted in Ryken, *Redeeming the Time*, 102.

God-glorifying; a poorly chaired one less so. An architect who imagines and incorporates beautiful features into his drawings is acting as an image bearer of the Creator. The nurse who applies the bandage with an empathy and precision that provides the experience of care and comfort in the midst of pain is reflecting God's compassion. The physicist who applies her formulas to contribute to our understandings of weather patterns is an image bearer of a wise God. When we do our jobs well, when we discover and apply all that God created and was "very good" in the garden of Eden for its intended purpose, we are bringing glory to our Creator. We are more accustomed to acknowledging the glory of God when we stand in awe at the majesty of unspoiled nature—be that on a mountain peak or at a waterfall—but God's glory is no less present and should be admired in the laboratory, boardroom, workshop, or soup kitchen where you might work. This world was created by and matters to God, and so does our work that takes place in this world. How can we say this? Let's go back to the Scriptures and unpack the basis for these claims in ten biblical principles.

GOD WORKS, AND WE ARE CALLED
TO BEAR HIS IMAGE

The ancient Greeks celebrated a life of contemplation and reflection as a higher form of work than menial labor. According to the philosopher Aristotle:

> It is true that both occupation and leisure are nec-
> essary but it is also true that leisure is higher than
> occupation, and is the end to which occupation
> is directed…. The feelings which play produces
> in the mind are feelings of relief from exertion;
> and the pleasure it gives provides relaxation. Lei-
> sure is a different matter: we think of it as having
> in itself intrinsic pleasure, intrinsic happiness,
> intrinsic felicity. Happiness of that order does not
> belong to those who are engaged in occupation:
> it belongs to those who have leisure. Those who
> are engaged in occupation are so engaged with
> a view to some end which they regard as still
> unattained.[8]

It seems that some Christians' notions of God
and His work are unduly influenced by ancient
Greek ideas. God is sometimes described as if He
were a divine clockmaker who made the world,
wound it up, and let it proceed on its own course.
From time to time, these Christians acknowledge
God in certain extraordinary events, much like the
Greeks, whose gods gathered in their councils to
determine the affairs of men. In the humdrum of
routine existence, however, they rarely reference
God's being and presence. But the Scriptures present a different picture.

In the opening verse of Genesis, God is actively
creating: "In the beginning God created the heaven

---

8. As quoted in Gilbert Mielaender, *Working: Its Meaning and Limits*
(Notre Dame, Ind.: Notre Dame University Press, 2000), 59.

and the earth" (1:1). In the final verse of Revelation, God is actively dispensing grace: "The grace of our Lord Jesus Christ be with you all" (22:21). In between, the Scriptures reveal to us a God who is active in His works of creation, providence, and redemption. The verbs used to describe God's activity throughout the Bible are active verbs—He is busy creating, speaking, showing, judging, planning, listening, laughing, and decreeing. In the midst of describing God's work, the psalmist breaks into a doxology: "Oh that men would praise the LORD for his goodness, and for his wonderful works to the children of men!" (107:15). Jesus, speaking to the Jewish leaders who were upset that He had healed a man on the Sabbath, noted, "My Father worketh hitherto, and I work" (John 5:17).

A biblical perspective of work starts with a biblical view of God. What is He doing, even today? Do not think of God as passively sitting on His throne, receiving the praises of His people and biding His time until judgment day arrives on the heavenly calendar. The Scriptures portray Him as actively working—using human analogies such as potter (Isa. 64:8), shepherd (Ps. 23:1), garment maker (Matt. 6:30), builder (Heb. 3:4), and composer (Zeph. 3:17)—to help our finite minds understand something of what He is doing.

It should also be noted that man, as God's image bearer, is allowed to emulate this characteristic: "Let us make man in our image, after our likeness: and let them have dominion over the fish of the sea, and over the fowl of the air, and over the cattle, and over all the earth, and over every creeping thing that creepeth upon the earth" (Gen. 1:26). The various animals were put on the earth with the expectation that they would follow their instincts, procreate, and live to God's glory. Man's task, however, is different. He was given dominion over the other creatures and is called to replenish and subdue the earth.

The connection between human work and divine work is made explicit when God gives the law on Mount Sinai: "Six days shalt thou labour, and do all thy work.... For in six days the LORD made heaven and earth, the sea, and all that in them is, and rested the seventh day: wherefore the LORD blessed the Sabbath day, and hallowed it" (Ex. 20:9, 11).

Leland Ryken summarizes the significance of this:

> Throughout the Bible, God is portrayed as an extremely active worker. In itself, this affects how we view human work. If God works, work is good and necessary. It is as simple as that. God's work is a model for human work, showing us that human work in the world is worth doing in a purposive, enjoyable, and fulfilling manner.[9]

The starting point for understanding human work begins with God. To be human, an image bearer of the Divine, is to be called to work.

---

9. Ryken, *Redeeming the Time*, 165.

GOD DERIVES SATISFACTION FROM HIS WORK

It is one thing to note the fact of God's work. It is even more instructive, however, to reflect on God's attitude toward His own work. It is clear from the Scriptures that God does not work because He has to, to fill the time, or for some other reason of necessity. God derives satisfaction and pleasure from the work of His hands. His work is fulfilling and meaningful.

Consider the creation account of Genesis 1. Each step of the way, we are told that God completed a task and took satisfaction from a job well done: "God said, Let there be light: and there was light. And God saw the light, that it was good" (Gen. 1:3–4). He separated the dry land from the water, "and God saw that it was good" (Gen. 1:10). The pattern repeats itself, and after each step the Scriptures note that God looks at what He has just accomplished and celebrates its goodness. The passage reaches a climax when the creation is completed: "And God saw every thing that he had made, and, behold it was very good" (Gen. 1:31).

Human analogies cannot capture the richness of God's satisfaction, and I do not mean to denigrate the perfection and completeness of God's work by comparing it to human actions. Still, I think we can learn something from an analogy. Think of something you are really good at. Perhaps you are a painter, and you have spent an entire evening behind an easel, painstakingly trying to convert the image in your mind onto the canvas. Or maybe you are a writer and are crouched over your desk, scratching away the words that don't quite say it the way you want and searching your mind to find the right one to complete your thought. And then, suddenly, like a light bulb flashing, it comes. "Ah ha! That's it!" you exclaim to yourself. "That's exactly what I was looking for." A flush of adrenaline flows through your body, and a feeling of satisfaction causes those muscles in your stomach to flex, and you breathe a little more deeply. It may last only a few seconds, but what a sensation it is to get it right, to know that what you have just completed is good work. It really doesn't matter how many people subsequently will admire your work and give you compliments; it really doesn't matter how much you may get paid for this project. There is no substitute for the feeling of satisfaction that comes in the moment when you know that what you have done is good.

The analogy breaks down in that sin impacts even our best work, and the process of accomplishing good work is a struggle and involves overcoming obstacles. None of this applies to the works of God. Yet the principle of this feeling of satisfaction is a reflection of what we read in the Genesis account. God sees the perfect creation—the birds, animals, fish, flowers, streams, and trees—with Adam and Eve diligently performing their tasks in Eden, and He, as it were, takes a moment at the end of His busy week of creation, surveys the scene, and thinks to Himself, "Behold, it is very good."

The Scriptures make note of God's pleasure in His work in other passages as well. The psalmist speaks of the Lord "[rejoicing] in his works" (104:31). Proverbs 8 portrays wisdom as created by God "from the beginning, or ever the earth was" (v. 23) and present with God throughout the creation process: "When he appointed the foundations of the earth: then I was by him, as one brought up with him: and I was daily his delight, rejoicing always before him; rejoicing in the habitable part of his earth; and my delights were with the sons of men" (vv. 29–31).

There are many passages of Scripture that highlight God's satisfaction in and taking pleasure in His own works. Let one more example relating to the work of redemption suffice here. In Ephesians 1, Paul describes the work of God with that well-known doxology of praise in which several times he mentions the pleasure God derives from this gracious provision:

Having predestinated us unto the adoption of children by Jesus Christ to himself, according to the good pleasure of his will. (v. 5)

Having made known unto us the mystery of his will, according to his good pleasure which he hath purposed in himself. (v. 9)

In whom we also have obtained an inheritance, being predestinated according to the purpose of him who worketh all things after the counsel of his own will: that we should be to the praise of his glory, who first trusted in Christ. (vv. 11–12)

God's work, whether of creation, providence, or redemption, is not a work of duty but a work of pleasure from which He derives satisfaction and glory.

GOD PROVIDES FOR US THROUGH OUR WORK

This does not mean, however, that the Scriptures speak of work only in existential terms. There is a tangible and practical side of work, in that the creation is structured in such a way that through our work our daily needs are met. When Satan appeared before God to discuss Job, he noted, "Thou hast blessed the work of his hands, and his substance is increased in the land" (Job 1:10). Job didn't achieve his riches by winning a lottery—it was as a result of his hard work that he achieved his wealth. The writer of Ecclesiastes makes a similar point:

> Behold that which I have seen: it is good and comely for one to eat and to drink, and to enjoy the good of all his labour that he taketh under the sun all the days of his life, which God giveth him: for it is his portion. Every man also to whom God hath given riches and wealth, and hath given him power to eat thereof, and to take his portion, and to rejoice in his labour; this is the gift of God. (Eccl. 5:18–19)

The point is uncontroversial, but we still need to consider it. In the order of creation, in the way

God put the world together, there is a connection between our work and receiving the necessities of life. This does not mean the relationship is automatic or that it is a mathematical relationship in that X amount of work will always reap Y amount of provisions. God is sovereign, and He is pleased to deal differently with our efforts. Sometimes they are richly rewarded—beyond what we can even imagine—while at other times it seems that the rewards are not at all proportionate to our efforts.

It is an almost natural temptation for us to pull God down to our level and try to sort through His blessings with some sort of human metrics. The Heidelberg Catechism reminds us that our work takes place in the context of the providence of God, which it describes in answer 27 as "the almighty and everywhere present power of God, whereby as it were by His hand, He upholds and governs heaven, earth, and all creatures, so that herbs and grass, rain and drought, fruitful and barren years, meat and drink, health and sickness, riches and poverty, yea, and all things come, not by chance, but by His fatherly hand." Even if the means by which God is ordinarily pleased to do this is through our daily work, we must remember that it is only God who can provide blessings upon our labors.

The tensions and anxiety that we face in connection with work belong to this life, but this does not mean that the connection between work and our provisions will not continue in the new earth. Isaiah provides a hint of this:

> And they shall build houses, and inhabit them; and they shall plant vineyards, and eat the fruit of them. They shall not build, and another inhabit; they shall not plant, and another eat: for as the days of a tree are the days of my people, and mine elect shall long enjoy the work of their hands. They shall not labour in vain, nor bring forth for trouble; for they are the seed of the blessed of the LORD, and their offspring with them. (65:21–23)

MAN WORKS IN OBEDIENCE TO GOD'S COMMANDS

An important point to recognize is that we must work because God has commanded us to. At creation, human beings were given the assignment to replenish the earth and subdue it. The creation pattern of work and Sabbath is repeated throughout the Scriptures. The Scriptures tell us not only that we must work but also how we must work. The command to work must be followed within the framework of God's other commandments. We are called to a life of total obedience, and there is interconnectedness between the various injunctions of Scripture. The command to work is captured in the summary of the law—namely, that we love the Lord our God with all our heart, soul, mind, and strength and that we love our neighbor as ourselves (Matt. 22:37–40).

It is useful to consider Exodus 31, a passage to which we will return later. Note the context. Moses was leading well over a million Israelites through the wilderness, from Egypt to the Promised Land. They stopped at Mount Sinai, and Moses received the two tables of the law and detailed instructions on exactly how to build the tabernacle. Lest Moses and Israel get carried away with their enthusiasm to complete this significant task, however, the Lord reminded them that this work—even though it was the work of building a house for the Lord—could be blessed only if it was fulfilled in the context of God's other covenant words:

> Six days may work be done; but in the seventh is the sabbath of rest, holy to the LORD: whosoever doeth any work in the sabbath day, he shall surely be put to death.... It is a sign between me and the children of Israel for ever: for in six days the LORD made heaven and earth, and on the seventh day he rested, and was refreshed. (vv. 15, 17)

The people were to understand and obey God's specific command to build the tabernacle within the more general framework regarding work and rest that God had established at creation.

GOD HOLDS US ACCOUNTABLE FOR OUR WORK

God gives each of us our tasks. The ability to complete those tasks is also a gift, and the only way there will be fruit on our labors is if God blesses us. The children of Israel were warned in Deuteronomy 8 not to succumb to the temptation of thinking that their work had earned all the material blessings they might enjoy: "Lest when thou hast eaten and art full, and hast built goodly houses, and dwelt therein… thou say in thine heart, My power and the might of mine hand hath gotten me this wealth. But thou shalt remember the LORD thy God" (vv. 12, 17–18).

Tithing and giving to the poor, in response to Old Testament commandments, caused the people to acknowledge that blessings came from God and were not earned through their work. The Levites and those in need were equally worthy of food as those who worked in the fields, and God expected to be acknowledged as the source of all blessing through regular tithes:

> At the end of three years thou shalt bring forth all the tithe of thine increase the same year, and shalt lay it up within thy gates: and the Levite, (because he hath no part nor inheritance with thee,) and the stranger, and the fatherless, and the widow, which are within thy gates, shall come, and shall eat and be satisfied; that the LORD thy God may bless thee in all the work of thine hand which thou doest. (Deut. 14:28–29)

Acknowledging that God, rather than our efforts, is the reason for earthly success is contrary to human nature. This is evident from the first pages of Scripture: Cain went from Eden, built a city, "and called the name of the city, after the name of his son, Enoch"

(Gen. 4:17). So much of our identity is caught up in our profession, and we are keen to take credit for the things we accomplish in our work. The Christian's only comfort in life and death is "that I am not my own but belong, body and soul, in life and death, to my faithful Savior Jesus Christ." We neither own our work, the gifts we possess that we use to work, nor the rewards that we are able to accumulate through our work. They are all gifts of God. Therefore, we ought to give honor and glory to God, who is the rightful owner of everything.

GOD PROVIDES PARTICULAR GIFTS TO MEET PARTICULAR NEEDS

I have already referenced Exodus 31 and God's command to Moses to build the tabernacle. Reading through Exodus 25–30, with all God's detailed instructions for the tabernacle and its various components, reveals the mammoth task that God gave Moses. It wasn't as if Moses had nothing to do! Leading an entire nation on a wilderness journey is a daunting task, and the challenges of governance, organization, and security also fell to him. And now a tabernacle had to be built according to very stringent specifications! How could this be accomplished? Where was Moses to find the resources? The Lord provides the answer:

> I have called by name Bezaleel the son of Uri, the son of Hur, of the tribe of Judah: and I have filled him with the spirit of God, in wisdom, and in

understanding, and in knowledge, and in all manner of workmanship, to devise cunning works, to work in gold, and in silver, and in brass, and in cutting of stones, to set them, and in carving of timber, to work in all manner of workmanship. And I, behold, I have given with him Aholiab, the son of Ahisamach, of the tribe of Dan: and in the hearts of all that are wise hearted I have put wisdom, that they may make all that I have commanded thee. (Ex. 31:1–6)

Bezaleel and Aholiab are not household names, even among those who are familiar with the Old Testament Scriptures. Yet they provide a wonderful example of how the Lord provides particular gifts to particular people to meet particular needs in His kingdom. If the skills inventories of modern human resource planning models were used to help Moses make his way through the wilderness, it is unlikely that the need for a stone and brass craftsman would have made the list. The point of the journey was not to stop and build but to get to the Promised Land. Aholiab was an expert in linen and specialty sewing. Possibly these two men were apprentices in Egypt and learned their craft from talented Egyptians; if that is the case, probably neither they nor their parents had any sense of God's providential purposes for their education. Yet when the Lord gives Moses the assignment, He also gives him skilled workers. Not only are Bezaleel and Aholiab available and gifted but they are also willing, as God has inclined their hearts. They are craftsmen filled with the spirit of the Lord, with wisdom and understanding to accompany their superior technical skills.

The gifts God provides us, however improbable it may seem to our human calculations, are given with a purpose and with providential insight, and we are called to use them in the service of God and His kingdom. There are no gifts that God gives to you and me by accident, even if the purpose and use of those gifts may not always be immediately obvious to us.

THE FALL'S IMPACT ON OUR WORK

The fall has radically impacted our work. Work has become toil, thorns and thistles frustrate our efforts, and fallen people seek to glorify themselves through their work rather than their Creator. With the fall came the curse, and the effect on work is profound:

> In sorrow shalt thou eat of [the ground] all the days of thy life; thorns also and thistles shall it bring forth to thee; and thou shalt eat the herb of the field; in the sweat of thy face shalt thou eat bread, till thou return unto the ground; for out of it wast thou taken: for dust thou art, and unto dust shalt thou return. (Gen. 3:17–19)

The Hebrew word translated "sorrow" in the King James Version and "toil" in various other translations is the same word used in verse 16 to describe the labor of childbirth. And it seems appropriate. The fall has radically affected both work and childbirth, so that we associate each process with significant pain. Yet there is something beautiful and God honoring that flows from these painful processes. The beauty of God's creation is marred, but the remnants of God's glorious creation and purposes can still be seen.

The writer of Ecclesiastes reminds us, however, that the reality of sin and the effects of the curse can dominate our work experience: "Then I looked on all the works that my hands had wrought, and on the labour that I had laboured to do: and, behold, all was vanity and vexation of spirit, and there was no profit under the sun" (2:11). "Yea, I hated all my labour which I had taken under the sun.... What hath man of all his labour, and of the vexation of his heart, wherein he hath laboured under the sun? For all his days are sorrows, and his travail grief; yea, his heart taketh not rest in the night. This is also vanity" (2:18, 22–23).

The curse of the fall does not just contribute to the drudgery and tediousness of work; it also has resulted in various vices and temptations particular to the workplace. For some, work is idolatry; others fall into the vice of laziness. The abuse of economic power is every bit as real and unjust as the abuse of military or political power. Dishonesty and deceit rear their ugly heads in the workplace. There are many opportunities for workers to point the finger of blame, reject authority, or cast covetous eyes on the rewards their coworkers or bosses achieve. Most of us can add personal details to the truth of what Solomon says: "I have seen all the works that are done under the sun; and, behold, all is vanity and vexation of spirit" (Eccl. 1:14).

When we confess our sins, do we confess the sins of the workplace? Is it not true that the ugliness of sin is particularly evident in our daily work and that our guard is often left down and we don't resist it? If we are honest with ourselves and submit to God's word, we realize how much the Holy Spirit needs to do His sanctifying work in us as we do our work in the face of the curse.

WORK IS BOTH INDIVIDUAL AND SOCIAL

In the opening chapters of Genesis, we are introduced to Adam's offspring. There was Jabal, the father of tent-dwelling cattle farmers (4:20); Jubal, the father of a family of talented musicians (4:21); and Tubalcain, who was the father of a family of brass and iron craftsmen (4:22). While this passage may be interpreted as saying there are certain tendencies and interests that are passed along through genetics, it also teaches that each of us does our work building on the work of others who have gone before us. Even Adam in his prefallen state did not have insight into all the technology that God had made possible in creation. It took learning, and each generation learned from the previous one. Also, there is development and progress in history in the way we work. Tubalcain was an "instructor of every artificer in brass and iron" (Gen. 4:22), suggesting that the ironworkers of early civilization received an apprenticeship under his watchful journeyman eyes.

The story of Scripture moves from the garden of Genesis 1 to the city of Revelation 22, and God has designed the world so that human work is an essential part of this process. Even Jesus was born into the world of technology as it existed two thousand years ago, and as He "increased in wisdom and stature, and in favour with God and man" (Luke 2:52), He learned from those around Him how to use the technology of His day. Whether He was using kitchen utensils or construction tools, Jesus had advantages over Adam in how he lived His everyday life and fulfilled His daily work. On the other hand, the twenty-first-century carpenter has tools that Jesus did not have available. Work is social as we interact in the workplace with our coworkers and teach and learn the specific skills of our discipline. There is also indirect interaction through intergenerational learning passed along through workplace practices as well as through textbooks.

This is an important principle that has implications for economic organization, a topic with tentacles far beyond our scope. Our work does not take place in a vacuum. Work by its very nature is generally accomplished in partnership with others. Adam received Eve as a helpmeet in Eden, and this pattern of working together is established in Scripture as normative.

GOD TAKES PLEASURE IN THE BEAUTY OF WORK

We naturally think of the economic dimensions of work, but it is important to emphasize that Scripture does not present work simply in its utilitarian function. We already have seen how God delights in His work and derives satisfaction from it not because of what it accomplishes, but for the sake of the work itself. The creation was good. But let's look a little closer. What was it about the creation that God noticed? Genesis 2:9 tells us that "out of the ground made the LORD God to grow every tree that is pleasant to the sight, and good for food." The modern workplace is organized around monetizing our work, so the price that can be obtained for the fruit compared to the value of the wood determines whether a particular orchard will be used for horticultural or forestry purposes. But that is not what this passage emphasizes. I don't want to read too much into it, but it is significant that the Scriptures mention the aesthetic appeal of trees even before mentioning their practical utility in providing for our needs. Psalm 19:1–2 reminds us of the role of creation in declaring "the glory of God." We serve a God who desires to be worshiped "in the beauty of holiness" (Ps. 29:2), and we are instructed whether "ye eat, or drink, or whatsoever ye do, do all to the glory of God" (1 Cor. 10:31). God is interested in everything we do and derives delight and pleasure from the beautiful as well as the functional.

One of my favorite passages of Scripture is Isaiah 46. After describing the foolishness of idol worship and serving the gods of our own creation, the Lord reminds His people, "I am God, and there is none like me" (v. 9). He then proceeds to describe His power and the certainty of His will, highlighting this with examples that to our finite minds seem unimportant but evidently from a divine perspective are essential: "My counsel shall stand, and I will do all my pleasure: calling a ravenous bird from the east, the man that executeth my counsel from a far country: yea, I have spoken it, I will also bring it to pass; I have purposed it, I will also do it" (vv. 10–12).

God derives pleasure not only from the obedience of men or the salvation of His people (as He expands on in the verses that follow) but also from the beauty of the flight of a bird. God pays attention to the raven that flies east, not just out of fatherly concern that the bird arrive safely at its destination, but with delight and pleasure. God notices and marvels at the beauty and splendor of the wings riding the air. He doesn't tell us which bird. But whether it is the majestic soaring hover of the eagle, the aerobic dive of the hummingbird, or just what seems to us an ordinary flight of a robin, God delights in them all. God loves beautiful things!

It seems safe to suggest that Scripture does not frame our work and the calling to work simply in terms of functional utility. As complex and diverse as we are as human beings, with various interests, aptitudes, and passions, so the work that we are called to is multidimensional. To reduce work to simply its economic or utilitarian dimension is to turn a blind eye to the splendid complexity that God has built into the creation, which He describes as "very good." Surely if we are to praise and glorify God as He deserves, we would do well to open our eyes to the various dimensions that are part of our daily work.

CHRIST WORKED AS PART OF HIS ACTIVE OBEDIENCE

The first principle I highlighted was the pattern of work as established by God and the satisfaction He derives from His work. The subsequent principles have attempted to show different dimensions of this pattern as revealed in Scripture. Perhaps your reaction to reading this is no different from mine in writing it; I cannot reflect on these truths without my conscience accusing me of falling so far short. In spite of my best efforts, my daily labors are often quite different from what I have been describing. I daily add to my mountain of sin by working in a manner that is so different from what the Scriptures require of us.

But, praise God, there is one more biblical principle that we cannot ignore. It is not enough just to look at work in the context of creation and the

fall; we also need to look at work in the context of
redemption.

Jesus too experienced work during His time on
earth. Whether we think of the learning He experienced as a child, His time in Nazareth as a carpenter,
or His work in the ministry during the final years of
His earthly life, He too had to obey God's law and
the command to work. When Paul writes that "by
the obedience of one shall many be made righteous"
(Rom. 5:19), we know that this obedience includes a
perfect fulfillment of God's command to work. When
we are troubled by challenges in the workplace and
our consciences accuse us of falling short yet again,
we know

> we have not an high priest which cannot be
> touched with the feeling of our infirmities; but
> was in all points tempted like as we are, yet with-
> out sin. Let us therefore come boldly unto the
> throne of grace, that we may obtain mercy, and
> find grace to help in time of need. (Heb. 4:15–16)

Cultivating biblical godliness in our work implies
an awareness of what we are called to do each day
when we go to work. To work is human. It is true
that animals also work in a sense, but it is something
very different from what we are called to do. Observe
the flurry of an anthill. It is an amazing expression of
God's creation. Yet the anthill's industry is different
from that observed in a human workplace. The col-
ony of ants carries out its task by instinct the same

way today as it has throughout history. There is no technology, progress, or development with the ants. It is God-glorifying in the sense that like the heavens, the ants declare the glory of their Creator. But there is no discovery, no learning, and no ability to consciously praise God in the anthill.

The work of humans, even in its most tedious forms, is so much different. We work in the conscious image of a God who works. Our creative energy and interaction with others cause us to grow in our knowledge, to discover new things in the creation the Lord has given us to steward, and to have a purpose beyond the survival instinct that motivates the animals. We are designed to praise our Creator, and as we work in a godly manner, we not only derive a certain satisfaction and sense of achievement (which, with a thankful spirit, is entirely appropriate) but even more so a sense of thanksgiving and praise for the God who has made us and called us to work.

Cultivating biblical godliness as it regards our daily work begins with understanding our work in a scriptural manner. Beginning each day with an intentional consciousness of what it is we are called to do and praying that God's Spirit may sanctify our motives, thoughts, and actions to conform us to His image, also in the workplace, orients us in a manner entirely different from most North American workers.

This is also a perspective that should inform how we speak about our work, including in a family setting. As we share our workplace stories at the dinner table, do our children hear only of the thorns and thistles, or do they also hear of the God-given delights we experience in our workday? While the cheerful acceptance of duty that Snow White's seven dwarfs display as they sing, "Heigh-ho, heigh-ho, it's off to work we go," is to be preferred over the more common "I owe, I owe" approach, neither captures the concept that believers should teach their children. The biblical narrative of creation, fall, redemption, and restoration should come through a balanced telling of our workplace stories. What did you discover in the course of your workday that causes a greater understanding of the creation, for which you give praise to the Creator? What about those difficulties you encountered? Do they cause you to hate sin and its curse more and more? Do we confess in prayer our sin and brokenness, as evidenced in the workplace? Do we take comfort from Christ's perfect work, both in obeying the law in His workplace experiences and also paying the price for our failures in His great redemptive work? At the end of each workday, do we not have new reasons to give Him thanks for this gracious gift? Do we work with advent expectation, recognizing that in the new earth we will work perfectly? Do we ever longingly and reverently contemplate what it will be to continue the discovery of creation and praise God for the amazing wisdom already present in the garden of Eden but that will continue to be revealed and come to fuller expression in that celestial city? If we were to regularly and intentionally share these per-spectives, making them concrete with examples from our particular vocation, we would instill a different understanding of work in the minds and hearts of our children.

VOCATION

We all face the question, how do I know what God is calling me to do? This is not only a question fac-ing young people considering their career options but also many people in the middle of a career as they consider whether to persevere through current work challenges or seek other opportunities. There are many factors to consider as we seek the Lord's will for our lives. Certainly we must consider our available opportunities, how best to provide for our families, and other legitimate concerns. Our culture tells us that we should make these kinds of decisions with personal reward and satisfaction in view, but a scriptural perspective on work implies that there are different factors we should incorporate as we make this decision.

Personally, I have found four questions useful in guiding career decisions.[10] They take into account not just our desires but also the uniqueness with which

10. These questions were inspired by and adapted from a lecture given by Gordon T. Smith in 1999. Subsequently, I read his book *Courage and Calling: Embracing Your God-given Potential* (Downers Grove, Ill.: InterVarsity, 1999), which developed some of these ideas further.

God has created each of us and the circumstances we find ourselves in.

First, what are your *gifts*? My parents could have told you when I was four years old that I was unlikely to be a mechanic or a carpenter. The sort of career that was suitable for me (as well as those that were not) was evident from my gifts, and honesty regarding our gifts (usually best achieved with the help of others) is a necessary starting point. We need to take care neither to fall into the trap of an exaggerated self-importance based on our gifts nor a false modesty that fails to account for what God has given us.

Second, what are your *passions*? Glorifying God through our work will come more easily when our work engages our passions. God loves what He does, and His work is an expression of His attributes. It is equally appropriate for those made in His image to recognize the different passions He has created in us. While sometimes what we love may align with our gifts and what we are good at, sometimes our passions and gifts are different, and it is helpful to be cognizant of both.

Third, what is your *temperament*? Some of us are people persons; others, not so much. Some of us need short-term rewards to maintain energy while others are better suited for long-term projects. It is not just the work itself but also the suitability of the pace and setting in which the work takes place that you should consider.

Finally, what are the *needs of God's kingdom*? The opening and closing of providential doors are certainly ways God makes His will clear to us. As we assess our options, however, it is important to examine our gifts not just in terms of the impact on our own career but also with regard to the broader needs of God's church and kingdom.

I am not trying to be comprehensive. Rather, I am pointing out that a biblical view of work intersects with a biblical view of vocation. Much of the worldly wisdom we receive on this topic runs counter to biblical principles.

CONCLUSION

We began with Perkins's four-centuries-old observation that the culturally dominant perspective of every man for himself and God for us all was a "wicked" perspective on vocation, counter to the biblical notion of our work being given to us by God for the common good. I have sought to establish from the Scriptures that doing our work well is to be human, in the most positive man-as-image-bearer-of-God sense of that word. To be sure, it is impossible in the brokenness of our fallen world to experience this as we ought. The curse is real, and we feel its effects daily. Add to that the selfishness and pride of our natural hearts; the idolatry of wealth, status, and prestige; and the inevitable challenges of relationships that belong to our workday experience, so that few of us find it easy to cultivate godliness in the workplace.

Praise God that the perfect righteousness earned by Jesus Christ is a complete righteousness that covers our daily work. But also keep in mind what a comfort the believer has, especially compared to the unbeliever. The vast majority of those who go to work each day with only self-satisfaction, earnings, or status as their motivation go home each night disappointed. There are many more losers than winners in the rat race of life. Many of our coworkers will confess that in the workplace they feel like a caged rat, going as hard as they can on the wheel but not really getting anywhere. Those who achieve progress and success find them disappointing, and the rewards fleeting.

By contrast, the believer with a biblically informed perspective goes to work each day with loftier expectations. Work is not about what we get from it. Rather, it is ordained by God, a place where we can use the gifts we have been given, discover more of the glory that He has embedded in His perfect creation, and be of use in His kingdom and to the benefit of our fellow human beings through the goods or services we provide. Yes, such lofty aspirations can result in disappointment when we realize how far short we fall. But even in our disappointment, we have reason for praise and thankfulness. As we confess in answer 63 of the Heidelberg Catechism, the perfect righteousness of Christ, as it pertains to our workplace obedience, is imputed to the believer. It is "as if I never had, nor committed any sin; yea, as if I had fully accomplished all that obedience which Christ accomplished for me, inasmuch as I embrace such benefit with a believing heart."

There is a familiar illustration, versions of which make it into many motivational speeches, about work and workplace culture. It resonates because it captures something of what work is intended to be in the created order. It is something that even those of a secular mind-set see as powerful, even if in practice they ignore it.

The story involves a visitor observing three men working on a construction site. He asks the first worker, "What are you doing here?"

"Can't you see, man? It's wet, miserable, and cold out here, and I have been at this since early this morning. These bricks are heavy, and the mortar is slimy. For weeks now, we have been on this project, putting stone on top of stone, row after row, over and over again. My hands are calloused and cut, my fellow workers are miserable, and my boss is a good-for-nothing you-know-what. I'm here to earn a paycheck, and believe me, what they are paying me isn't enough!"

The second worker's response is more positive. "I am in the final year apprenticing to be a mason. Another six months, and I will have my ticket and plan to start my own business. I am persevering and making something of my life, and working on this project will be an important part of my resumé."

The visitor proceeds to the third worker. "What are you doing here?"

With a beam of pride breaking through the grime on his face and a wave of his hand toward the sparse frame that outlines the beginnings of a building beyond the wall, the workman responds, "Can't you see, sir? We are building a cathedral!"

Each of us is called by God through the gifts He has given, in the providential circumstances He has arranged, to contribute to His kingdom. May God bless us each day as we build cathedrals to His glory!